To the future Queen or King may you be inspired with this story to be a leader that will serve with justice for all. You have been chosen to lead, you are special and you are blessed. Jesus loves you so much.

"Let the little children come to me, and do not hinder them, for the Kingdom of God belongs to such as these" -Jesus

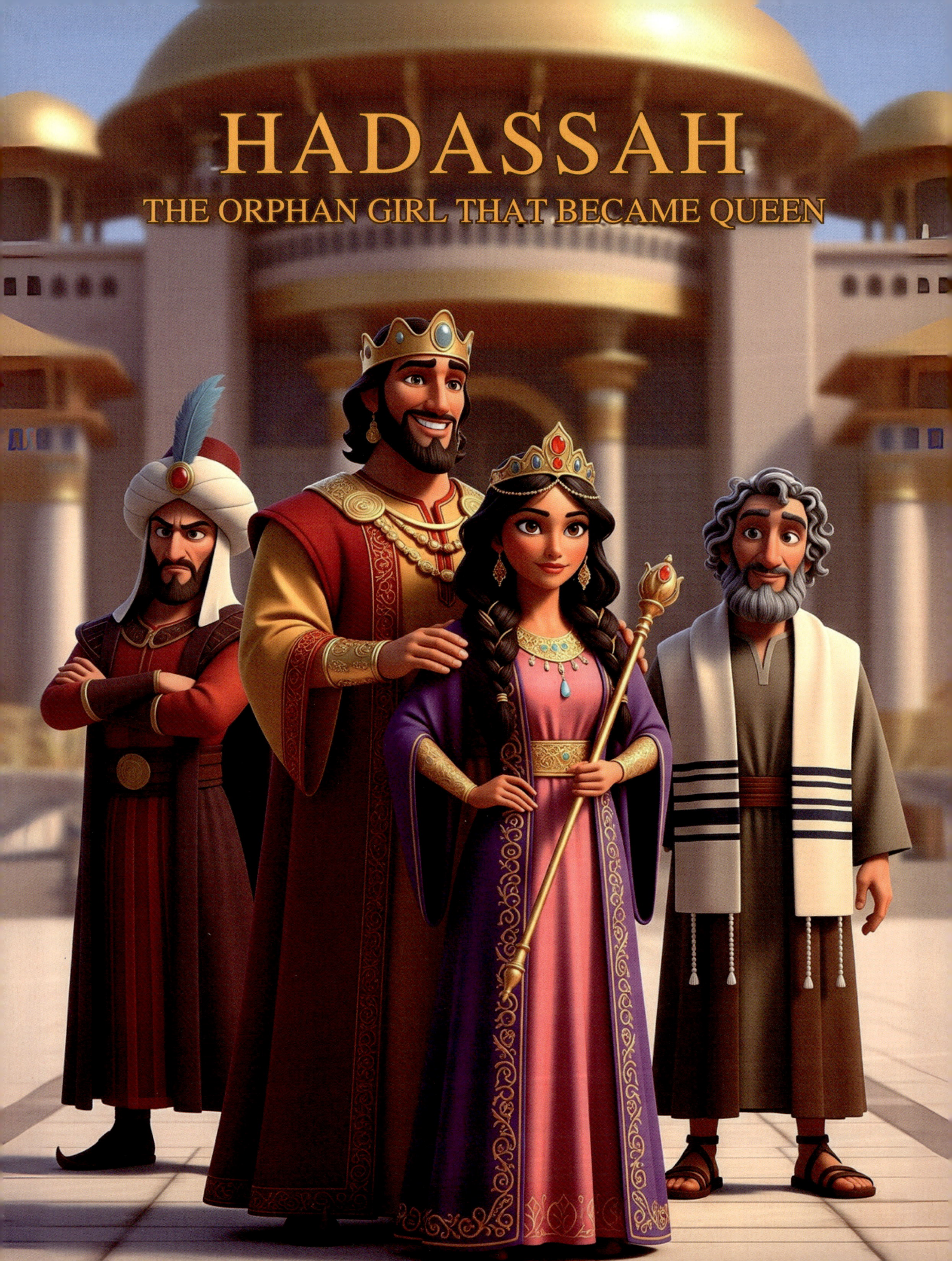

HADASSAH

THE ORPHAN GIRL THAT BECAME QUEEN

In the city of Shushan, there lived a kind girl named Hadassah. Her parents had passed away when she was very little. Her older cousin, Mordecai, took care of her and raised her like his own daughter. They were Jews and lived a simple life.

The ruler of the land was King Ahas. He ruled 127 provinces. His wife, Queen Vashti, refused to come when he called her during a big party. The king became very angry and said she could no longer be queen.

After many months, King Ahas chose Hadassah to be queen. He gave her a new name, Esther, and had a big party to celebrate. Esther now lived in the palace, but she still remembered everything Mordecai had taught her.

One day, Mordecai heard two palace workers talking about a bad plan to hurt the king. He told Queen Esther, and she told the king. The king stopped the bad plan and kept Mordecai's help written in his royal book.

Later, the king chose a man named Haman to be the most important leader. Everyone had to bow to him, but Mordecai would not. Haman got angry and made a terrible plan to destroy all the Jews, including Mordecai.

When Mordecai heard the plan, he wore torn clothes and cried in the streets. Esther heard about it and sent a servant to ask why. Mordecai begged her to ask the king to save their people. Esther said, "Tell everyone to fast and pray for 3 days."

After 3 days, Esther put on her royal clothes and bravely went to see the king. The king was happy to see her and said, "What do you want, Queen Esther?" She invited him and Haman to a special dinner.

That night, Haman told his wife and friends he was happy to eat with the king and queen. But he said, "I can't be happy while Mordecai is alive!" His wife and friends said, "Build a tall gallows and ask the king to hang him." Haman liked the idea and built it.

That same night, the king couldn't sleep. He read the royal book and saw that Mordecai had saved his life. The next day, the king made Haman honor Mordecai in front of everyone. Haman was upset, but he had to do it.

At the second dinner, Esther told the king, "Haman wants to destroy my people." The king was shocked and very angry. He ordered Haman to be punished on the tall gallows Haman had built for Mordecai.

The king gave Haman's things to Esther and made Mordecai a great leader. A new message was sent to all 127 provinces to protect the Jews. The people were saved! They had a big celebration called Purim, and it is still celebrated today.

PRAYER

Heavenly father, I come before you today to thank you for always watching over me, thank you for my family and friends. I pray that you forgive me for where I have been disobedient to my parents, teachers and leaders. Help me Lord to be a better person, to obey your word, my parents, teachers and leaders. Teach me how to better serve my family and country. Lord bless my family, friends and Country. Let thy will be done in my life as it is written in heaven so that you will get all the glory. In Jesus name I pray believing and trusting. Amen.

The End